IMAGES
of America

MINNEAPOLIS'S
LAKE STREET

IMAGES
of America

MINNEAPOLIS'S LAKE STREET

Iric Nathanson

ARCADIA
PUBLISHING

Published by Arcadia Publishing
Charleston, South Carolina

Printed in the United States of America

Library of Congress Control Number: 2019948887

For all general information, please contact Arcadia Publishing:
Telephone 843-853-2070
Fax 843-853-0044
E-mail sales@arcadiapublishing.com
For customer service and orders:
Toll-Free 1-888-313-2665

Visit us on the Internet at www.arcadiapublishing.com

To Marlene.

CONTENTS

ACKNOWLEDGMENTS

I owe a very large vote of thanks to the people who worked with me to put together this pictorial history. Two long-time Lake Street experts, Allison Sharkey and Cara Letofsky, reviewed my early drafts and offered useful suggestions that helped me tell the Lake Street story in a fuller, more complete way. Ted Hathaway and his staff at the Hennepin County Public Library Special Collections located many of the archival images I was able to use in the book. Eric Mortensen at the Minnesota Historical Society and Carol Fong at the Northwestern Architectural Archives helped me access the extensive archival collections maintained by their two organizations. Angel Hisnanick, my editor at Arcadia Publishing, kept me on track as this project moved from the idea stage to the final product. And finally, my wife, Marlene, provided support and encouragement during those long hours that I spent hunched over my computer as *Minneapolis's Lake Street* came together. All images are courtesy of the Minnesota Historical Society unless otherwise noted.

INTRODUCTION

As it cuts across South Minneapolis from one end of town to the other, Lake Street reflects the city's diversity and its rich history. At its western end, the street curves around one of Minneapolis's most prized natural amenities, a lake recently renamed to honor the native people who once lived along its shores. Beyond the lake, this six-mile thoroughfare heads straight east, ending at the Mississippi River.

Lake Street's origins extend back to the late 19th century when it was a dirt road separating farm sections out beyond the Minneapolis city limits. But the road would soon emerge as a key transportation route when it became an access point for a bridge across the Mississippi connecting Minneapolis with St. Paul after the turn of the last century. As South Minneapolis underwent an economic and population boom during the early decades of the 20th century, Lake became a magnet for commercial development up and down its six-mile length.

That development was concentrated at key commercial nodes where Lake was intersected by a series of north-south arterial streets. Lake and Hennepin, known as Uptown by the 1930s, became the retail center for a collection of upscale neighborhoods surrounding the city's lakes. Six blocks to the east, the Lyndale intersection was the site of Lake Street's first "skyscraper," the five-story Calhoun Building, constructed in 1913. Farther down Lake, Nicollet Park was the home of the Millers, the city's professional baseball team for a half century, up through the mid-1950s.

At Lake Street and Chicago Avenue, the massive Sears Roebuck development was built in phases starting in 1927. Its 16-story tower soon became Lake Street's dominant landmark.

Beyond Chicago Avenue, Hiawatha Avenue, adjoining a major railroad line, was an early industrial hub and the site of a major farm implement manufacturing plant. Nearby Twenty-Seventh Avenue emerged as a major retail center, rivaling Uptown at Lake Street's western end.

In between the major nodes, Lake Street filled in with hundreds of retail shops, restaurants, offices, and more than a dozen movie theaters. By the 1950s, Lake Street had become Minneapolis's auto row, home to new car dealers and small used car lots.

But soon, Lake Street's role as a major automotive district began to fade as the car dealerships started abandoning South Minneapolis and relocating in the suburbs. One by one, the movie theaters began to close or were converted to tawdry "porn palaces." By now, Lake Street was succumbing to the forces of suburbanization, which were draining the economic energy out of inner-city commercial districts all across the country.

Lake Street's decline was accentuated by the impact of Interstate 35 West, which cut a broad swath through the city starting in the late 1960s. As the suburban boom gained momentum, the interstate tended to depress commercial activity along the South Minneapolis corridor by neglecting to include a southbound freeway access point at Lake Street. The thoroughfare's problems were compounded by an ill-advised decision by city officials to block off Nicollet Avenue at its intersection with Lake. Nicollet was closed at Lake Street in order to entice a national chain to locate a retail outlet at that site.

Lake Street, particularly its midsection between I-35 West and Hiawatha Avenue, struggled to combat the forces of urban decay during the final decades of the last century. That struggle was highlighted by the murder of a Minneapolis police officer at a Lake Street café in 1992. The murder contributed to an escalating crime wave that caused the *New York Times* to label Minneapolis "Murderopolis." Then in 1994, Lake Street suffered another blow when Sears closed and its massive complex was abandoned.

Despite these setbacks, the seeds of Lake Street's renewal were planted when an energetic group of new arrivals, many from Mexico and Latin America, began moving into South Minneapolis. Later they were joined by newcomers to Minnesota from East Africa. These aspiring entrepreneurs started renovating Lake Street's deteriorating storefronts for their family-owned businesses. By the early 2000s, more than 100 Latino businesses were located along Lake Street, many in the thriving Mercado Central at the Bloomington intersection.

Lake Street's fortunes received a major boost when the vacant Sears complex was redeveloped and repurposed as the Midtown Exchange in 2005. The multi-use project was anchored by Allina Health and its corporate offices. The 16-story Sears tower was converted to condominiums and apartments. The adjoining two-story structure that had housed the Sears retail store became an innovative global market, used to incubate neighborhood-based businesses, many owned by new arrivals and people of color. The market was developed by a consortium of nonprofit organizations led by the St. Paul–based Neighborhood Development Center. Just beyond the Midtown Exchange, a local arts organization rescued the shabby Avalon Theater and converted it to a home for its Heart of the Beast Puppet and Mask Theater.

By the end of the 21st century's second decade, Lake Street's western end at Uptown was undergoing a frenzied real estate boom, while the thoroughfare's eastern end, beyond Hiawatha Avenue, was developing in a more measured manner. Throughout its six-mile length, a revitalized community organization, the Lake Street Council, helped guide Lake Street's emerging role as a strong, vibrant commercial corridor.

One

EARLY ERA

At the turn of the 20th century, Lake Street was still a narrow dirt road surrounded by open fields. "During the rainy and thawing periods, it was almost impassable," the *Minneapolis Journal* noted. "In summer it was heavy with dust. There were wooden sidewalks only in certain sections." But this modest roadway was about to undergo a major transformation. In 1905, the Twin Cities Rapid Transit Company (TCRT) started running a streetcar along Lake Street, extending out to the Wonderland Amusement Park, which opened that same year. In 1906, the new Lake Street Bridge opened, enabling TCRT to establish its intercity Selby Lake line, linking Lake Street with St. Paul's Selby Avenue.

Streetcars were now traveling across the bridge, but Lake Street had still not been paved. "Lake Street from Minnehaha Avenue is in a fearful condition, making it impossible for people either to drive or walk," the *Journal* reported in May 1906. "Property brought with the intention of improving and building had to be put on hold until the road was put in passable condition." Developers and real estate speculators didn't have to wait long. Within a few years, Lake was paved from one end of the roadway to the other, unleashing a development boom that would continue through the early decades of the 20th century. Initially, people living near Lake Street had opposed the plan for the intercity streetcar line, but "the die was cast," according to the *Journal.* "Lake Street's destiny seems to point to commerce. In the opinion of real estate men and property owners, it will mainly be a business street."

The *Journal's* prediction proved to be accurate. By 1913, nearly 350 businesses had located along Lake Street between Hennepin Avenue and the river. One of those was Schatzlein's Saddle Shop, Lake Street's oldest existing business, established in 1909. The South Minneapolis shop outfitted horses at a time when much of the land south of Lake Street was still being used for farming.

Even before the Selby-Lake streetcar line opened in 1906, rail lines extending out from the city's downtown core had reached Lake Street. By the turn of the last century, a real line along Nicollet Avenue brought baseball fans out to Nicollet Park, the home of the city's professional baseball team, the Minneapolis Millers.

The first two decades of the 20th century witnessed the rapid growth of Lake Street's key commercial intersections at Hennepin, Lyndale, Nicollet, Chicago, and Twenty-Seventh Avenues.

In the 1880s, noted landscape architect H.W.S. Cleveland urged the Minneapolis Park Board to create a 200-foot-wide boulevard connecting Lake Calhoun to the Mississippi River. Cleveland's boulevard would have followed the route of modern-day Lake Street. While the board did implement Cleveland's plan for the "Grand Round" of parkways connecting the city's lakes, it rejected his proposal for a Lake Street boulevard. Lake remained a narrow, unpaved roadway into the early years of the 20th century.

The Minneapolis Park Board built its first bathhouse at Lake Calhoun in 1890. Surging use by summer crowds prompted the board to build a new bathing facility on Calhoun's shore at Lake Street. According to Minneapolis historian David Smith, when the new bathhouse opened in 1912, "lines of people waiting for a place to change clothes extended for blocks on the hottest days."

Initially, the park board established dress codes for Lake Calhoun bathers, including a requirement that women's bathing costumes, as they were known, reach six inches below the knee. But not everyone at the lake had come there to swim. These well-dressed onlookers were not dressed in bathing attire.

By the 1910s, more bathers were able to bypass the bathhouses because they were walking to the lake or arriving by car. "The bathing suit habit has extended even to those living many blocks from the lake and fortunate enough to own an automobile," the *Minneapolis Tribune* observed in early August 1914. "The sight of a machine filled with bathing suit clad people is almost as common today as are the machines themselves."

The Minneapolis Park Board achieved a long-sought goal in 1911 when it built a lagoon connecting Lake of the Isles with Lake Calhoun. This cartoon shows the "marriage" of the two lakes that occurred that year on July 5 at opening ceremonies for the park board project. During the ceremony, water from each lake was mixed together in a golden goblet and deposited in the lagoon.

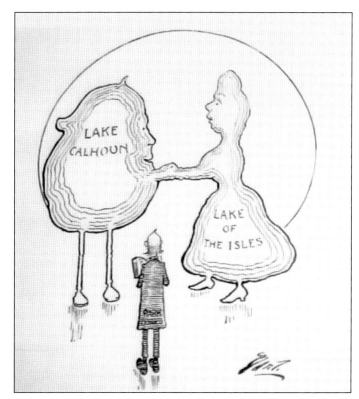

The festivities culminated with a parade of decorated canoes through the lagoon following a small boat carrying dignitaries making the first trip through the channel linking the two lakes. The project required the park board to build a series of bridges over the channel, including the one shown here. (Courtesy of Hennepin County Library Special Collections.)

Over a four-year period from 1912 through 1916, the Lake Street corridor was substantially upgraded when the railroad line along Twenty-Ninth Street was rebuilt and lowered into a three-mile-long trench. The reconstruction project was intended to eliminate the numerous accidents caused by the original rail line that crossed nearly 50 South Minneapolis streets at grade. In later years, the rebuilt rail line would provide the right-of-way for the Midtown Greenway.

The Walker Community Library at Twenty-Ninth Street and Hennepin Avenue brought branch library services to rapidly growing neighborhoods on the city's west side. The building, which opened in 1911, was the first of three Walker libraries at that intersection. T.B. Walker, considered the father of the Minneapolis library system, donated the site for the branch library that bears his name.

The new West High School attracted a crowd of more than 2,000 well-wishers when it was formally opened on September 25, 1908. The three-story building at Twenty-Eighth Street and Hennepin Avenue contained 75 rooms and an auditorium seating 1,000. During its first year, West served more than 1,000 students from the city's west side neighborhoods.

Grand Opening Performance
LAGOON THEATRE 3
SATURDAY EVENING, JUNE

HENNEPIN AVE.
NEAR LAKE ST.

HENNEPIN AVE.
NEAR LAKE ST.

The Finest Photoplay
Theatre
in Minneapolis

To make this beautiful
theatre as pleasant and comfortable as possible for our
patrons we have spared no expense in the selection of fixtures and conveniences. The best approved style of chairs have been installed which insure rest and comfort.

The ventilating system is the best and is being used by the largest theatres in the country.

Special Attention
to the
Comfort of Women
and Children

Visit this beautiful theatre on its opening day. You will at once be attracted by the unique arrangements of every facility for comfort and pleasure—all with the idea in view of making it pleasant and convenient for women and children.

Our aim at all times shall be to Please Our Patrons.
Rest and Enjoy Yourself

Full Orchestra at ALL Performances
THE PICTURES WILL BE THE BEST
You will be able to view your favorite Film Star at the LAGOON. We are going to show only the Best First Run Films—right when they are NEW.
EVERY FILM THE BEST SELECTION
We are choosing from the most interesting, most instructive, and most entertaining Film Services in the country. Watch our announcements.

First Performance at 7 p. m.   Matinees Every Afternoon
10c — Popular Prices of Admission — 10c

The Lagoon was one of a group of early movie houses built along the Lake Street corridor during the second decade of the 20th century. They included such long-gone names as the American, the Bungalow, the Cort, and the Idle Hour. One of South Minneapolis's largest movie theaters at the time, the Lagoon could seat 1,000 patrons. Later renamed the Uptown, the Lagoon was the only Lake-area theater to survive into the 21st century.

LAKE STREET AND HENNEPIN AVENUI

Where Lake Street Joins the Lakes—Where Traffic Never Ceases

PROMINENT TENANTS IN OTTAWA BLOCK

American State Bank, Rudolph Heck, Druggist, Dr. McBride, Dentist, Thompson's Bakery and McNally, Tailor, Occupy Practically Entire Building.

In a 1916 article, the *Minneapolis Tribune* commented on the growing number of businesses locating in the Hennepin-Lake commercial district: "With its rapid growth and prosperity, Hennepin has grown to be one of the busiest corners of Lake Street." The *Tribune* noted that the new businesses included the American State Bank. "The establishment of a banking institution in this vicinity is an indication of the rapid growth and prosperity of the district."

On Lake and Hennepin's southeast corner, two brothers, Nick and John Geanakoplos, put up a retail and office building that housed their Lake View Confectionery. "The store has gained considerable attention by reason of its beautiful fixtures," the *Tribune* reported. "As vendors of fine candies, ice cream, sodas and flowers, the Geanakoplos brothers stand second to none." In the 1980s, the facade of the Geanakoplos building was incorporated into Uptown's new urban-style shopping center, Calhoun Square. (Courtesy of Ray Harris.)

One of Lake View's major competitors, Abdallah's Candies, was diagonally across the street on the northwest corner of Lake and Hennepin. The firm's founder, Albert Abdallah, a native of Lebanon, operated the confectionery with his Swedish-born wife, Helen Trovall. While Abdallah's is no longer located on Lake Street, the 110-year-old business is still family owned and operated by Albert Abdallah's descendants.

When Abdallah's first opened, the store was "a source of pride to the residents of this locality," the *Minneapolis Tribune* reported in 1916. "The fame of the ice cream manufactured by the Lathrop Kemp Company and sold to Mr. Abdallah has grown so that it now requires a wagon load a day to suffice." These Abdallah employees were kept busy serving their hungry customers.

The oldest public building in the Hennepin-Lake district, Calhoun School at Lake Street and Girard Avenue, opened in 1887. As the neighborhood continued to grow during the early decades of the 20th century, the school was enlarged in 1904 and again in 1920. After the school was demolished in 1973, the site was incorporated into a new retail development.

Lake Street and Lyndale Avenue developed as an important commercial intersection before the turn of the 20th century. The intersection, known as Lyndale Corners, connected Lyndale Avenue, the city's major north-south thoroughfare, with Lake Street. A streetcar line along Lyndale linked Lake with downtown Minneapolis as early as 1891, boosting Lyndale Corners' development potential.

The five-story Calhoun Building was Lake Street's only "skyscraper" when it opened in 1913. Calhoun Bank occupied the building's street level, while the upper floors contained professional offices and a ballroom. One hundred years later, the Calhoun Building continues to serve as a professional office building.

These well-dressed fans were watching a hard-fought battle between the Minneapolis Millers and the St. Paul Saints at Nicollet Park in 1904. Eight years earlier, in 1896, the Millers played their first game at their new home field at Nicollet Avenue and Lake Street. Nicollet Park served as the home of the Millers until 1955. That year, the South Minneapolis ballpark was torn down. The next season, the Millers moved to a new open-air stadium in Bloomington.

St. Mary's Greek Orthodox Church was originally located on the University of Minnesota campus. This domed building on Lake Street served as the congregation's second home from 1910 through 1956. St. Mary's moved to its current location overlooking Lake Calhoun in 1957.

The massive seven-story Boyd warehouse dominated the intersection of Fourth Avenue and Lake Street when it was built in 1910. Constructed to serve as a storage facility, the building advertised its fireproof construction on its façade facing Lake Street. Now Northstar Mini Storage, the former Boyd warehouse continues to serve the same function today as it did in 1910.

Originally known as Layman's Cemetery, the Minneapolis Pioneers and Soldiers Cemetery on Lake Street dates to 1853. The cemetery serves as the final resting place for about 200 military veterans who fought in conflicts ranging from the War of 1812 to World War I. In 2002, the Pioneers and Soldiers Cemetery was listed in the National Register of Historic Places.

The Pioneers and Soldiers Cemetery was built on land originally owned by Martin Layman, an early Minneapolis settler. In 1852, Layman arrived in what was then the Territory of Minnesota. He received a permit from the authorities at Fort Snelling to stake a claim to land on the west side of the Mississippi River, then part of the fort's military reservation.

In 1910, the Twin Cities Rapid Transit Company built its Lake Street Station at Twenty-First Avenue as a repair, maintenance, and storage facility for its fleet of streetcars. The sprawling facility included a series of indoor tracks flanked by an inspection pit. The station replaced a smaller TCRT shop at Bloomington Avenue.

Minneapolis Steel and Machinery Company was one of the Lake Street corridor's earliest industrial firms. The company was formed in 1902 to manufacture metal products used in a broad range of industrial machinery. In the 1920s, Minneapolis Steel and Machinery merged with two other firms to create Minneapolis Moline, one of Minneapolis's largest industrial firms and a key Lake Street fixture through the 1970s.

During World War I, Minneapolis Steel and Machinery's products were in high demand. With many of its male workers off to fight in France, the company began to hire women to work on the shop floor for the first time. This photograph shows them in their one-piece work clothes.

Longfellow School, dating to 1887, replaced an earlier school that was outside the Minneapolis city limits when it was built in 1876. Longfellow was one of the first schools in Minneapolis to offer a kindergarten class. The 1887 building was later demolished and replaced by the current Longfellow School on East Thirty-First Street. (Courtesy of Hennepin County Public Library Special Collections.)

One of the oldest Lake Street–area buildings still in use today, Fire Station 21 was built in 1894. During its early years, the station relied on the use of soda acid extinguishers that could contain fires until more fully equipped steamers and hose wagons arrived on the scene. Fire Station 21 remained in operation until 1961. In more recent times, the building has been used as a furniture store and a cabaret theater.

In 1888, Martinus Nelson built a blacksmith shop near the corner of what is now Minnehaha and Lake. Ten years later, a Danish immigrant named Christian Lauritzen took over Nelson's shop and expanded it. Lauritzen continued to operate the shop at its original East Lake location until 1946. The building was demolished in the late 1980s to make room for a parking lot.

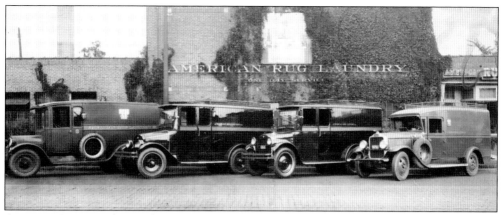

American Rug Laundry is Lake Street's oldest business still operating at its original location. The company opened in 1918 as an international influenza epidemic was gaining momentum. The October 1918 ad below told prospective customers they could "guard against influenza" by getting their rugs cleaned. By the end of the year, the epidemic had subsided, but not before claiming the lives of more than 7,000 Minnesotans.

Wonderland was an amusement park at the east end of Lake Street, in operation from 1905 to 1911. When Wonderland opened for a second season in 1906, the new Lake Street bridge helped boost attendance. "Now people living in St. Paul can reach the park as handily as those from Minneapolis," the *Minneapolis Journal* noted in May 1906. The park's focal point was an illuminated 120-foot tower that could be seen throughout South Minneapolis. (Courtesy of the Longfellow Community Council.)

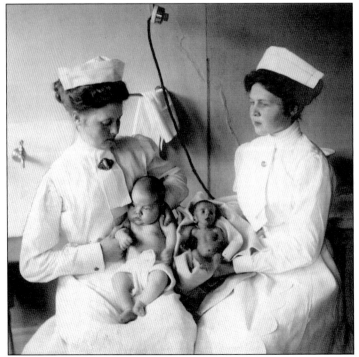

Wonderland was also the site of a small hospital for premature babies. While the hospital was located on the Wonderland grounds, it was not considered a park attraction. Instead, the hospital was intended to promote the use of a new system of infant incubation. The hospital was the only structure that survived Wonderland Park's demolition in 1911. It is now an apartment building on Thirty-First Street, one block south of Lake Street

The South Minneapolis amusement park was a popular summer attraction over its six-year life. The young men in the photograph at right may have just finished riding Wonderland Park's roller coaster. That same day, they may have also dashed down the Shoot the Chutes, an early form of water slide, later adapted for more modern amusement parks.

Streetcar service came to Lake Street in 1905, boosting the street's role as a major commercial thoroughfare. The Selby-Lake Line, as it was later known, used Lake Street as the connection between St. Paul on the east and the Minneapolis suburbs on the west. "Lake Street's destiny seems to point to commerce," the *Minneapolis Journal* observed a month after the service began, "In the opinion of real estate men and business owners it will be mainly a business street."

With the completion of the Lake Street bridge in 1906, the Twin City Rapid Transit Company was able to use the bridge to provide streetcar service across the river into St. Paul. But Lake Street itself was still unpaved, impeding auto travel on the roadway. "Improvement and building had to be held back until the roadway was put in a passable condition," the *Minneapolis Tribune* reported. That happened in 1913 when Lake Street was fully paved.

Two

EMERGING CORRIDOR

At the turn of the 20th century, European immigrants were flocking to Minneapolis, attracted by the city's booming economy. Large numbers from Scandinavia settled in the modest neighborhoods surrounding the downtown retail district. By the 1920s, many of these first- and second-generation Minnesotans began moving out from the inner-core districts to the newly developed neighborhoods along Lake Street. Charles Ingebretsen, a native of Norway, was part of that movement. Ingebretsen opened his first grocery store in the heavily Scandinavian Cedar Riverside neighborhood before relocating to East Lake Street.

During the post–World War I era, Lake Street began to fill in with scores of small businesses whose storefront names proclaimed the Scandinavian origins of their owners. Lake remained a corridor of small, family-owned firms until 1928, when the mammoth Sears development opened on a four-acre site just east of Lake Street and Chicago Avenue. Sears's 16-story tower would become Lake Street's most notable landmark.

In 1930, just as the "talkies" were starting to upend Hollywood, Lake Street, home to nearly a dozen movie theaters, had become South Minneapolis's "Great White Way." That year in January, moviegoers could see Harold Lloyd's first talking comedy, *Welcome Danger*, at the Granada, later renamed the Suburban World. Down the street on Hennepin Avenue, Joan Crawford talked for the first time in *Untamed* at the newly upgraded Uptown.

Throughout the 1930s, Lake Street theaters provided a respite from the Great Depression for thousands of working-class families in the South Minneapolis neighborhoods. But those neighborhoods did not feel the full force of the Depression, according to Wallace Freeman, whose family operated Freeman's Department Store at Twenty-Seventh and Lake Streets. "Many of the people who lived there still had jobs at the Ford plant and at Minneapolis Moline," Freeman recalled. "They were Swedes and Norwegians who were by nature thrifty. They didn't waste their money." While retail stores in other inner-city neighborhoods were forced to close during the 1930s, Freeman's was able to survive and grow. Freeman's retained its role as South Minneapolis's major department store well into the 1970s.

This ad in the February 28, 1920, edition of the *Minneapolis Tribune* promoted Lake Street's retail businesses. "You couldn't wish for more ideal conditions to shop than are found on Lake Street," the paper declared. "There is the absence of the crowds downtown—you are not jostled and pushed around." The *Tribune* noted that the population of the Lake Street district had increased by 80 percent since 1910.

In 1923, when plans were unveiled for the upscale Calhoun Beach apartment hotel overlooking Lake Calhoun, its promoters promised to provide "the Northwest's finest and most beautiful hotel for those who desire a beautiful lake home without the responsibility and care of its upkeep." But the plans kept getting delayed until the ambitious project was stalled following the stock market crash of 1929. After standing empty for a number of years, the Calhoun Beach hotel finally opened in 1946.

In 1930, the Minneapolis Park Board constructed this building on the north end of Lake Calhoun, which served as an open-air dining hall or refectory and the home of the Lake Calhoun Yacht Club. For nearly 90 years, the refectory was a popular lakeside gathering spot. In 2019, a fire destroyed the landmark building.

This West Lake building was originally known as the Joppa Temple. It was designed by a Minneapolis architect, Clyde W. Smith, for the Joppa Lodge of the Masons. Now known as the Citadel, the former Joppa Temple is an Uptown office building. (Courtesy of Hennepin County Public Library Special Collections.)

The Minneapolis Arena was an indoor ice and roller rink at Twenty-Ninth Street and Dupont Avenue. Over a 40-year period from the 1920s through the mid-1960s, the arena hosted hockey games and ice shows. The popular Shipstad and Johnson's Ice Follies, shown below, performed in the arena between 1936 and 1966. The Minneapolis Arena was later torn down to make room for a Rainbow Foods store. (Both, courtesy of Hennepin History Museum.)

Originally a movie theater known as the Calhoun, the Uptown Ballroom, at Lake Street and Girard Avenue, became the center of social life for the west side neighborhoods in the 1920s and 1930s. The ballroom was a popular gathering spot for young people during Minneapolis's jazz age. These musicians broadcast live from the Uptown Ballroom on WRHM, a CBS network affiliate that later became WTCN radio. The Uptown Ballroom building is now the home of Stella's Fish Café.

In 1928, the Granada Theater opened at Lake Street and Hennepin Avenue, one block south of the earlier Lagoon Theater. The Granada's elaborate façade was intended to give the theater a Spanish revival feel. In 1954, the Granada became the Suburban World. For the next 40 years, the Suburban World continued to show second-run movies until it closed in 1994. For a short time in the early 2000s, the theater reopened as the Suburban World Cinema Grill. In 2019, the former Granada Theater is scheduled to become a music and event venue.

In May 1922, Schlampp's Furrier opened a South Minneapolis retail store and production facility, relocating from its earlier location on West Broadway. In this *Minneapolis Tribune* ad, the store declared that its new building at Hennepin and Lagoon Avenues was "built to our own specifications, especially planned for the most satisfactory display and storage of fine furs." During its 80 years on upper Hennepin Avenue, Schlampp's was a center of high fashion in Uptown. The store closed in the early 2000s.

IN READINESS—
Schlampp's Splendid New Fur Salon

A BUILDING of our own; built to our specifications, especially planned for the most satisfactory display and storage of Fine Furs. This building is the embodiment of the ideals we have held during the eighteen years of our experience in the fur business in Minneapolis. We want you to see our new home. It's ready now. You'll find it well worth a visit. You will find Schlampp fur values as consistently low as always—and quality the finest. Manufacturing our own furs and being out of the high rent district makes our substantial savings possible.

Schlampp's New "Extra Proof" Fur Storage Built as an integral part of this splendid fire-proof building, the new Schlampp Storage Vaults are kept at a temperature of 15 to 36 degrees by an elaborate refrigeration system. Fresh air is constantly forced to every part of the vaults by electric fans. Two feet concrete walls and heavy metal doors make damage by fire or loss by theft impossible. Yet the charge for this "Extra Proof" storage is astonishingly reasonable.

PHONE DYKEWATER 1871—WE WILL CALL FOR YOUR FURS

One Block Below Lake Street

P. Schlampp & Son
Established 1904
MANUFACTURING FURRIERS
2919 HENNEPIN AVENUE
(Formerly 911 26th Ave. North)

This industrial building on Lake Street between Dupont and Colfax Avenues served as the headquarters of the Buzza Company between 1923 and 1942. At its high point, the Minneapolis firm was the country's second-largest manufacturer of greeting cards, with 300 employees at its Lake Street plant. After Buzza shut down in 1942, the building was purchased by the federal government and used to manufacture precision optical equipment for the US Army. The Buzza Building, now known as the Buzza Lofts, has been converted to affordable rental housing. (Both, courtesy of Hennepin County Public Library Special Collections.)

PORT ARTHUR CAFE.

"The Best Chow Mein in Town"

9th ANNIVERSARY
Special

FREE DELIVERY anywhere in city **APRIL 13-23**

Including Country Club, St. Louis Park and Richfield Districts.

CHOW MEIN FOR TWO ONLY _____50c

Our Chow Mein is nourishing, tasty and wholesome. Order your next Chow Mein from us. You'll enjoy it.

PORT ARTHUR CAFE

PL easant 2421   **1427 W. LAKE**

The Port Arthur Cafe was one of more than a half dozen Chinese restaurants located along the Lake Street corridor at one time. In this 1940 ad, the restaurant advertised chow mein for two for 50¢. The Port Arthur remained an Uptown fixture for more than 50 years.

Standard Heating is shown here at its West Lake Street location. The company was established in 1930 by Tony Ferrara, who began his working career as a furnace repairman. Standard Heating, now located on Plymouth Avenue in North Minneapolis, is still owned by the Ferrara family.

Although its identity has changed over the years, the Crowell building at Lake Street and Lyndale Avenue has anchored that intersection for more than 130 years. The building gets its distinctive look from the band of bay windows at the second-story level. The down-at-the-heels Lake Street Café on the building's first floor was later replaced by a popular Greek restaurant that closed in 2019.

Lake Street's oldest existing business dates to 1907, when Emil Schatzlein began building saddles in a small shop on West Lake. The photograph below shows Emil in 1920. Today, Schatzlein Saddle Shop is still owned and operated by Schatzlein family members. (Both, courtesy of Schatzlein Saddle Shop.)

Sears, Roebuck and Company purchased and demolished 46 buildings at Elliot and Lake to make room for its mammoth new Minneapolis complex. The *Minneapolis Tribune* noted that the buildings were "all sacrificed in the name of progress." Construction of the new Sears center took over two years in 1927 and 1928. (Courtesy of Hennepin County Public Library Special Collections.)

The $5 million Sears development covered a four-acre site on the north side of Lake Street between Chicago and Tenth Avenues. Its 16-story tower would soon become a major South Minneapolis landmark. The development included a retail store fronting Lake Street and distribution center for 800,000 mail order customers. (Both, courtesy of Hennepin County Public Library Special Collections.)

As the city's first auto-oriented shopping center, Sears provided a free parking lot for its customers on the west side of its building. The Minneapolis lot was modeled after a similar facility at the company's retail store in Chicago. In later years, the city of Minneapolis designated the Sears parking lot as a historic site because of its early connection with auto-oriented retailing. (Courtesy of Hennepin County Public Library Special Collections.)

In the early 1920s, Charles Ingebretsen and his partner, Al Olson, opened a store at Sixteenth Avenue and East Lake Street. The business, known as Ingebretsen's Model Market, included a meat market and grocery store. Today, Ingebretsen's is still in its original East Lake location. One of Lake Street's oldest family-owned businesses, Ingebretsen's is still operated by Charles Ingebretsen's descendants. (Both, courtesy of Julie Ingebretsen.)

Charles Ingebretsen is shown here (seated at center) chairing the Bloomington Lake Civic Association. In its 1929 profile, the *East Lake Shopper* noted, "Mr. Ingebretsen has established his business and personality on the principles of fair value exchange. His recognized leadership, both in commercial and social fields, indicates his dual grasp on intrinsic personal fundamentals." (Courtesy of Julie Ingebretsen.)

These streetcars are crowded together at Lake Street Station, waiting for their next run. With its 25 tracks covering a full city block, Lake Street Station was able to accommodate 180 cars. The station provided storage and maintenance for streetcars traveling along the Selby-Lake line and other South Minneapolis routes.

Minneapolis Moline was established in 1926 through the merger of three farm implement manufacturing firms—Minneapolis Steel and Machinery, Minneapolis Threshing Machine Company, and the Moline Implement Company. The merged firm continued to produce tractors at its Minneapolis plant on Lake Street until 1972. The plant was later demolished and replaced by a retail center anchored by a Target store.

In 1917, E.B. Freeman moved his haberdashery shop from its original location on Twenty-Sixth Avenue to a new building on East Lake Street known as the Coliseum. Freeman and his wife, Harriet, who managed the store's women's department, built their family business into one of Minneapolis's largest department stores outside of the downtown core. Freeman's Department Store closed in 1975, a victim of the suburban boom that was overpowering inner-city retailing all over the country.

Freeman's was a major advertiser in the *East Lake Shopper*, a South Minneapolis community newspaper published from the early 1930s through the mid-1950s. In this 1941 ad, Freeman's advertised women's spring coats starting at $3.95. The store announced that it would accept relief orders at a time when the economy was still feeling the lingering effects of the Great Depression.

This Minneapolis branch library opened in 1924. It was built to serve the rapidly growing residential neighborhoods along East Lake Street. The 1924 branch was eventually replaced by a modern library just down the block on Lake Street. The original library building has been converted to a warehouse and retail outlet for a Lake Street business.

Holy Trinity Church traces its history to 1904 when a group of young people in Minneapolis broke away from a Danish-speaking congregation because they wanted to use English in their services. After worshiping in temporary quarters for a number of years, the congregation built this church in 1925. In more recent years, Holy Trinity has developed housing for the elderly and for people with special needs on property adjacent to the 1925 building. (Courtesy of Holy Trinity Church.)

Luke Rader, an early radio evangelist, established his River Lake Gospel Tabernacle at Forty-Sixth Avenue and East Lake Street in 1928. Rader's son Paul also preached at the Lake Street church. The Raders laced their fiery sermons with strongly anti-Semitic messages. The building was demolished in 2002 to make room for a mixed-use retail and housing development at that site.

Three

ACTIVE YEARS

As the Great Depression began to ease in the late 1930s, Lake Street businesses thrived. The advent of World War II brought larger pay envelopes to workers at the local defense plants, but Lake's several dozen grocery stores and their customers were soon caught up in wartime food rationing. At Lake Street's western end, a newly-built market, Hove's, opened just before the start of the war. Hove's later evolved into the Twin Cities' premier supermarket chain.

Several miles away, the East Lake manufacturing plants retooled for wartime production. Along with farm implements, Minneapolis Moline began producing jeeps for the US Army. Lake Street area residents who went across the river to work at the Ford Plant soon found themselves building M-8 armored vehicles rather than Ford sedans.

Through the 1930s and into the 1950s, the area's movie theaters brought huge crowds to the Lake Street corridor. Several theaters, including the Uptown and Rialto, received Art Deco makeovers during these years. At Nicollet Avenue and Lake Street, the Minneapolis Millers continued to draw thousands of baseball fans until the team's home field, Nicollet Park, closed in 1955.

Lake Street boomed during the 1950s and into the 1960s when the area's auto dealers attracted eager car buyers from all over the Twin Cities. But Lake Street's identity as Minneapolis's auto row would soon fade.

People living along the Lake Street corridor were able to go about their daily business using a streetcar network extending throughout the metro area. The Selby Lake line ran across town from the Mississippi River to Hennepin Avenue. North-south streetcar lines crossed Lake Street at Nicollet, Chicago, Cedar, and Twenty-Seventh Avenues.

The area's trolley car era ended when the Twin Cities Rapid Transit Company eliminated streetcars in 1954 and replaced them with buses. The end of that era meant the closing of the company's Lake Street Station at Twenty-First Avenue. The massive streetcar repair and maintenance facility was later replaced with an auto-oriented strip mall, the Hi-Lake Center.

This aerial view of the Hennepin-Lake district in the mid-1930s was part of a series of aerial photographs commissioned by the Minneapolis Board of Education. The numbers on the photographs mark the locations of Minneapolis public schools. West High School is noted with a "1," and Calhoun school is marked with a "2." The multistory building at the top of the photograph is the headquarters of the Buzza Company. (Courtesy of Hennepin County Public Library Special Collections.)

By 1938, Uptown had become the city's largest commercial district outside of downtown. More than 100 small retail businesses were located within a two-block radius of Hennepin Avenue and Lake Street. They included five gas stations, seven cafes, six grocery stores, and two movie theaters.

This billboard at Lake Street and Hennepin Avenue signaled Lake Street's role as a major auto dealership corridor during the middle decades of the 20th century. At its high point in the 1940s and early 1950s, Lake Street's "auto row" was the home of more than 20 dealers. By 1980, they had all abandoned Lake Street and relocated to the suburbs.

When Hove's opened at Lake Street and Irving Avenue in 1939, it was one of the city's first self-service grocery stores. The store was built by Russell Lund, a partner in the business. In 1964, it was renamed Lund's. Russell Lund and his family later built Lund's into one of the Twin Cities' largest grocery chains. Now known as Lunds & Byerlys, the Lake Street store is still in operation at its original location.

The family-owned Rainbow Cafe was a South Minneapolis institution for 60 years. The café at Lake Street and Hennepin Avenue was established by Christ Legeros in 1919 and later operated by his sons until they sold the business in 1979. The Rainbow was known for its extensive menu and late-night hours. (Courtesy of Hennepin County Public Library Special Collections.)

The Uptown Theater had not yet received its Art Deco makeover when it caught fire on April 25, 1939. The fire, which started in the ventilating system, was quickly brought under control by the Minneapolis Fire Department, but the plume of smoke pouring off the building brought a crowd of spectators to the site. The 1939 fire set the stage for the Uptown's extensive renovation later that year.

The Uptown is Minneapolis's only movie theater from the early 20th century still in operation today. With its landmark tower, the theater continues to anchor the busy Hennepin Avenue and Lake Street commercial district. The rebuilt theater was designed by Minnesota's leading Art Deco–era architectural firm, Liebenberg and Kaplan. (Courtesy of the Northwestern Architectural Archives.)

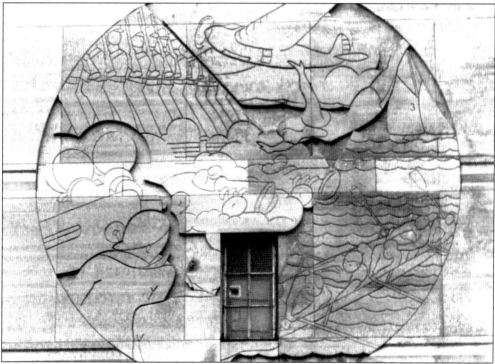

This decorative relief sculpture was added to the façade of the Uptown Theater when it was rebuilt in 1939. The sculpture was designed by Gustave Kollman, an Austrian-born artist best known for his Northern Pacific Railway posters. Kollman has incorporated a movie camera image in his circular design, along with references to nearby Lake Calhoun.

Babe Ruth gives a young fan some pointers during a visit to Nicollet Park in September 1935. Ruth had come to Minneapolis to participate in a benefit game between the Minneapolis and St. Paul Police Departments. "The Babe played the whole nine innings, but didn't hit a home run," the *Minneapolis Tribune* reported. "The crowd that spilled on to the field after the game didn't seem disappointed and the autograph business was as brisk as ever." (Courtesy of Hennepin County Library Special Collections.)

The Minneapolis Millers are warming up during a pre-game practice at Nicollet Park in 1941. That year, the Millers, under manager Tom Sheahan, placed fourth in the American Association standings, behind the Columbus Red Birds, Louisville Colonels, and Kansas City Blues. (Courtesy of Hennepin County Public Library Special Collections.)

Fans hurry into Nicollet Park to watch the Minneapolis Millers play their final game in the South Minneapolis ballpark on September 28, 1955. At that game, fans were rewarded with a Miller victory when the Minneapolis team defeated the Rochester Red Legs, winning the Junior World Series Championship. Two months later, the historic ballpark on Lake Street was demolished. (Courtesy of Hennepin County Public Library Special Collections.)

This ad for Ingebretsen's Market appeared in the *East Lake Shopper* on December 26, 1941, just a few weeks after Pearl Harbor and the start of US involvement in World War II. Within a few months, Ingebretsen's and grocery stores all across the country would be caught up in the federally mandated food-rationing system. The ubiquitous ration books would be a part of daily life in the United States during the war years.

During its heyday as Minneapolis's auto row in the 1930s and 1940s, Lake Street was the home of nearly two dozen auto dealers. While the new car dealers eventually abandoned Lake Street and relocated to the suburbs, the corridor's smaller used car lots like this one at Lake and Portland Avenue remained well into the 21st century.

In 1936, Nate Roberts opened the shoe store that bore his name on the northwest corner of Lake Street and Chicago Avenue. Roberts Shoes continued to anchor that intersection for more than 70 years. Roberts passed the family-owned business to his son-in-law Mark Simon, who continued to operate the shoe store until 2014.

After its Art Deco makeover, the Rialto Theater staged its grand reopening on August 12, 1937. For its opening, the Rialto showed *Kid Galahad*, starring Edward G. Robinson and Bette Davis. At the time, a local community newspaper described the Lake Street movie house as the "Twin Cities newest, most beautiful suburban theater." But that description no longer applied by the 1970s, when the Rialto had become a neighborhood eyesore. The theater closed in 1990. (Left, Courtesy of Hennepin County Public Library Special Collections.)

Louis Grossman established his Chevrolet dealership on Lake Street in 1920. Initially, the fledgling business had only three employees. But later, it would become one of the largest Chevy dealerships in Minnesota. When Louis Grossman retired, his son Harold took over management of the family-owned business. In 1978, Harold Grossman moved Grossman Chevrolet to Burnsville. (Courtesy of the Grossman family.)

Peter Soteropolos operated a candy shop at Lake and Bloomington before opening Cedar Lake Floral in 1932. In 1948, Cedar Floral reopened after undergoing a major remodeling. Later, Soteropolos's sons Ted and Nick took over the family business. Cedar Floral closed in the early 2000s.

As American industry geared up for a wartime economy in 1942, Minneapolis Moline began producing jeeps for the US Army. In a wartime ad, the company noted that "Minneapolis Moline engineers started work on the original jeep now accepted by our armed services even before the global war broke out. Already hundreds of MM jeeps are in use by the armed forces and more are going in steadily." This photograph shows two Army officers inspecting Moline's Lake Street plant.

Minneapolis Moline workers were able to purchase war bonds through a voluntary payroll deduction plan established at the Lake Street plant in 1942. Moline's CIO Union Local 1146 was a cosponsor of a war bond rally held at the Minneapolis Auditorium. With a workforce of 4,100, Minneapolis Moline had the second-highest number of defense workers in the Twin Cities, only trailing New Brighton's Northern Pump, which had 4,600 workers at that time.

On August 20, 1945, disgruntled workers at Minneapolis Moline's South Minneapolis plant blocked traffic on Lake Street for 20 minutes as they launched a strike that lasted nearly two months. Workers and their union claimed that the company was unfairly withholding the final paychecks of laid-off workers unless those workers signed a release waiving seniority and other union rights. The protest occurred less than a week after VJ Day, August 15, which marked the end of World War II.

During its early years, the Toro Manufacturing Company built tractor engines on a contract basis for the Bull Tractor Company. The Minneapolis-based company, located at East Lake Street and Snelling Avenue, took its name from the Spanish word for bull. Later, Toro started building mowers and other lawn maintenance equipment under its own name. In 1962, the Lake Street business moved to suburban Bloomington. (Both, courtesy of the Toro Company.)

Hi-Lake Shopping Center was built on the site of the former Lake Street Station, a streetcar hub operated by the Twin City Rapid Transit Company. The center's initial tenants included a Red Owl grocery, a Walgreen's drugstore, and several other retail chain outlets. Extensively remodeled in recent years, Hi-Lake Center continues to serve as a Lake Street retail anchor.

The Odd Fellows building at Twenty-Seventh Avenue and Lake Street was engulfed in flames on October 28, 1948, when an oil spill ignited in the building's basement. Spectators watched as flames shot out the windows and the roof collapsed. After a six-hour battle, the fire was finally subdued by 150 firemen who brought half the city's firefighting equipment to the blaze.

The Town Talk Diner was a popular lunch spot for workers from the nearby Minneapolis Moline plant. When the plant closed in the early 1970s, the Town Talk fell on hard times. The restaurant closed in 2002, and the space remained empty until it reopened in 2006 as an upscale eatery. Since then, the Town Talk has gone through several remakes, but its original lighted sign remains a popular East Lake landmark.

The Brown Institute was originally known as the American Institute of the Air when it was established in 1946. During its 50-year history on Lake Street, it trained generations of radio and TV broadcasters. This building, at 3123 East Lake Street, served as the headquarters for the Brown Institute from 1957 until the school moved to a new building at 2225 East Lake Street in 1986. That location is now the site of Hennepin County's L&H Station development. (Courtesy of Pavlik Museum of Broadcasting.)

Ostrom's marine and sporting goods store at Lake Street and Thirty-Sixth Avenue was in the national spotlight for a time in 1962. That year, in its August 17 issue, *Life* magazine featured a story about a Finnish-made Rapala fishing lure sold at Ostrom's. The story, entitled "The Lure that Fish Couldn't Pass Up," resulted in a rush of business for the Lake Street shop The store's owner, Ray Ostrom, was later inducted into the Fisherman's Hall of Fame for his efforts to popularize the Rapala lure. (Courtesy of Cathy Ostrom Peters.)

In 1934, Elmer T. Anderson established his Chevrolet dealership at Thirteenth Avenue and West Lake Street. Later, Anderson moved his business to a new Lake Street site at Forty-Second Avenue. In 1958, he sold the business to Harold Larson, who renamed the dealership Harold Chevrolet. The former Anderson Chevrolet building is now occupied by Northwest Graphics Supply.

Four

CHALLENGING TIMES

The decade of the 1970s was a challenging time for Lake Street, but one area business made the decision to expand during those years. In 1974, Ingrebtsen enlarged its food market at Sixteenth Avenue to include a Scandinavian gift shop. While Ingebretsen's was expanding, the corridor's auto dealers were abandoning Lake Street. Grossman Chevrolet, a Lake Street fixture for more than 50 years, was one of the last to leave. In 1978, Grossman announced it was moving to Burnsville.

Five years earlier, the Lake Street industrial manufacturing era came to an end when Minneapolis Moline closed. After its plant was demolished, the Moline site was redeveloped into a new retail center.

Lake Street suffered a sharp blow when the Sears store, a longtime area landmark, closed in 1994. The Sears complex would remain empty for more than 10 years, casting a blighting shadow on the nearby neighborhoods.

During the 1990s, neighborhood activists battled to combat prostitution, pornography, and urban blight along the Lake Street corridor. Despite the challenges facing Lake Street during these years, the corridor did experience some development, particularly at Lake and Hennepin, where a new urban-style shopping center was constructed within the shell of one of the district's historic buildings.

Lake Point condominiums opened in 1978 at the corner of West Lake Street and Dean Boulevard. The 25-story building overlooking Lake Calhoun was the first in a series of high-rise projects that sparked opposition from area residents who objected to what they saw as excessive development of the city's lakefront. The controversy led to height restrictions for future lakefront projects. (Author's collection.)

In 1962, a Minneapolis-based fraternal group, the Sons of Norway, constructed this Lake Street office building, which served as the organization's headquarters. The building also housed the Fifth Northwestern National Bank (later Wells Fargo), which had moved from its original location on Hennepin Avenue. In 2018, the Sons of Norway building was demolished to provide a site for a new mixed-use development. (Courtesy of Ray Harris.)

Calhoun Square, an in-town retail development, opened in 1984 on the southeast corner of Hennepin Avenue and Lake Street. The $16 million project included an indoor shopping mall that incorporated the façade of the historic Geanakopolos Building, constructed in 1917. During its planning stage, the city-backed development generated opposition from some neighborhood residents who maintained that the project was out of scale with the surrounding residential neighborhoods.

These photographs show the second of three buildings constructed to house the Walker Library. Once described as "a library for book worms who like to burrow," the second Walker Library, which opened in 1981, was sunk into its site in keeping with the architectural trend at that time for underground buildings. It replaced the original 1911 Walker Library across Hennepin Avenue. The underground Walker Library was demolished in 2013. A new Walker Library now occupies that site. (Both, courtesy of Hennepin County Public Library Special Collections.)

Uptown held its first art fair in 1964. Since then, the fair has been held each year during the first full weekend in August. The three-day event attracts several hundred thousand visitors who shop for paintings, sculpture, jewelry, ceramics, and other artworks offered by more than 300 artists and craftsmen. The Uptown Art Fair is sponsored by the Uptown Association. (Courtesy of Hennepin County Public Library Special Collections.)

In 1977, Minneapolis closed off Nicollet Avenue between Twenty-Ninth Avenue and Lake Street as an enticement to get Kmart to locate a store there. Officials justified the action, maintaining that the street closing provided Kmart with the footprint it needed for one of its big-box stores. Later, city leaders acknowledged that the street closing had been a mistake because of its chilling effect on businesses along upper Nicollet Avenue.

When business and community leaders learned about the street closing, they organized a protest group, Keep Nicollet Open (KNO), to block the project. KNO tried unsuccessfully to persuade Kmart to locate on a site adjacent to Nicollet Avenue that would have kept the street open. Curt Brown, one of the group's leaders, is shown above protesting the project.

NICOLLET
BASEBALL PARK

* · *

For 60 years -- 1896 through 1955 -- Nicollet Park, located in this block, rang with the cheers of Minneapolis Miller baseball fans. Spectators came from all across the upper midwest to watch the best baseball in the region. On one occasion it was reported that the entire town of Buhl, Minnesota -- 530 people -- motored down to the city to watch the Millers play. The park drew its largest crowd ever on April 29, 1946, when 15,761 people watched a double header between the Millers and the St. Paul Saints. The seating capacity of the park was 8,500. The Saints won both games.

Many of baseball's big names played and managed at Nicollet Park, some for the Millers and some as visitors. Among them were Ted Williams, Hobe Ferris, Perry Werden, Mike and Joe Cantillon, Joe Hauser, Gene Mauch, Hoyt Wilhelm, Rube Waddell, Rosy Ryan, Bill Rigney, Herb Score, Al Worthington, Donie Bush, Mike Kelley, Spencer Harris, Ray Dandridge, and Willie Mays.

This plaque on the former site of the Minneapolis Miller's home field reads, "Nicollet Park, located in this block, rang with the cheers of Minneapolis Millers baseball fans. Spectators came from all across the upper midwest to watch the best baseball in the region." (Author's collection.)

The Nicollet Park site was later incorporated into the city's Nicollet Lake Redevelopment Project. As part of the project, a Northwestern National Bank branch was built on the former ballpark block. Northwestern's weather ball on top of the building forecast the weather. Today, the bank is part of the Wells Fargo system.

In the early 1960s, the Minnesota Highway Department began building a leg of Interstate 35 West that cut through Minneapolis from north to south. As they began planning for the new urban freeway, highway officials opted to run I-35 West on a bridge over Lake Street rather than building an interchange there. Many South Minneapolis community leaders believe that the decision to bypass Lake Street contributed to its decline as a major commercial corridor.

Neighborhood residents picketed the Chicago Lake Bookstore in 1985, protesting what they saw as the store's unhealthy effect on the Chicago Avenue–Lake Street intersection. The bookstore and the adjacent Rialto Theater were owned by Ferris Alexander, who operated other pornographic businesses in Minneapolis, including the store pictured below at Fourth and Lake. (Left, courtesy of the *Star Tribune*; below, courtesy of Hennepin County Library Special Collections.)

At one time, the Rialto Theater was one of South Minneapolis's most popular entertainment venues. However, by the 1980s, the Rialto had become a shabby "porn palace." Community activists were eventually able to rid themselves of the Rialto and the adjacent Chicago Lake Bookstore. The neighborhood trouble spots were demolished to provide a site for the Lake Street office of the Minnesota Department of Employment and Economic Development.

Sears made several efforts to keep up with the times during its final years on Lake Street. In 1988, the retail chain's Lake Street store underwent a major remodeling. The building overhaul included this new 3,500-square-foot coffee shop, seating 350 customers. This update did little to halt Sears's decline. The store closed in December 1994 and remained vacant for the next 10 years.

In 1978, Grossman Chevrolet announced that it was relocating to a site in suburban Burnsville. "You always hate to leave the old home," the dealership's owner, Harold Grossman, said as he was preparing for the move. Grossman claimed that his inner-city location put him at a competitive disadvantage with other auto dealers in the Twin Cities. "Lake Street is no longer an automobile street," Grossman told the *Star Tribune*. The former Grossman Chevrolet building is now known as New York Plaza.

In 1974, Ingebretsen's, a longtime South Minneapolis landmark, expanded its Lake Street store to include a Scandinavian gift shop. The gift shop was organized by Julie Ingebretsen, Charles Ingebretsen's granddaughter. "We opened the shop at a time when Lake Street was beginning to face difficult times," Julie noted, "But the slide started so slowly. We really didn't notice it back then." (Author's collection.)

On September 25, 1992, Jerry Haaf, a Minneapolis police officer, was shot and killed while sitting in the Pizza Shack restaurant on Lake Street. Three local gang members were later tried and convicted of the slaying. The Pizza Shack incident helped highlight Minneapolis's growing crime problem in the 1990s. Minneapolis honored Haaf by naming a city-owned parking ramp for him. (Above, courtesy of the *Star Tribune*; below, author's collection.)

Highway 55, which follows the route of Hiawatha Avenue, cuts across Lake Street on this bridge. The roadway was rebuilt after a decades-long dispute over the highway alignment was finally resolved. In 2019, plans were underway to redesign the Hiawatha intersection to make it more pedestrian-friendly.

After Ohio-based White Motor Company purchased Minneapolis-Moline, the new owner decided to close Moline's Lake Street plant along with a second plant in Hopkins. The factory closings put more than 1,200 Moline employees out of work. The last Moline tractor rolled off the Lake Street shop floor on June 9, 1972.

Target's Lake Street store opened in 1976. A year later, the Minnehaha Mall opened at an adjacent site. Both projects were part of a city-assisted effort to redevelop the former Minneapolis Moline site. The development generated opposition from community activists who wanted the city to maintain the site for industrial rather than retail use. The activists maintained that industrial development would provide more living-wage jobs for neighborhood residents. (Author's collection.)

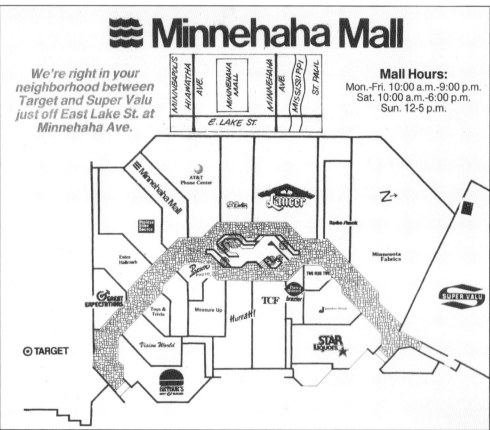

When it opened in 1977, the Minnehaha Mall billed itself as the first indoor shopping center in Minneapolis built within the previous 15 years. The mall's suburban configuration, fronting on a large parking lot, would soon fall out of favor with urban planners who wanted to discourage auto uses and promote higher density development. This diagram shows the project's initial tenants.

When the new Third Precinct police station opened in 1985, it was the first new police station built in Minneapolis in 30 years. The station featured a public entrance facing the corner, designed to be open and accessible to the community, according to the building's architect, Jack Boarman. The 1985 building replaced an earlier police station on Twenty-Seventh Avenue, demolished as part of the Twenty-Seventh and Lake Street development project. City hall officials are shown below at the opening ceremony for the new station. (Right, author's collection; below, courtesy of Lake Street Council.)

Construction began on a new Lake Street bridge in 1989. One year later, on April 29, 1990, an arch for the new bridge collapsed. Robert Moser, a construction worker at the site, was killed when the arch fell into the Mississippi River. After the damage was repaired, construction resumed. The rebuilt Lake Street bridge opened in 1992. (Courtesy of the *Star Tribune*.)

Five

THE 21ST CENTURY

The foundation for Lake Street's revival was set in place during the late 1990s when a group of nonprofit community organizations came together to promote small business development along the corridor. Their work was supported by a newly energized Lake Street Council, a community organization representing new and established businesses along the corridor.

In 1999, aspiring entrepreneurs from Latin America were the driving force behind an early revitalization effort on Lake Street. Their work led to the creation of the Mercado Central, a central market at Lake and Bloomington that provided space for several dozen small retail businesses.

The next major development along Lake occurred in the early 2000s when the vacant Sears complex was repurposed as a mixed-use commercial, housing, and retail center. Now known as Midtown Exchange, the development provided office space for Allina Health adjacent to the health care corporation's flagship medical facility, Abbott Northwestern Hospital. Sears's landmark tower was converted to condominiums and rental apartments. At Lake Street, the former Sears retail store was rebuilt for the Midtown Global Market, a retail center housing more than 50 small businesses. The market was developed by a group of community-based nonprofit organizations led by the Neighborhood Development Center.

In 2004, the region's first light-rail transit line began operating. Now known as the Blue Line, it connected downtown Minneapolis with the Mall of America. One of the Blue Line's major stations, located at Lake Street and Hiawatha Avenue, helped boost Lake Street's role as a key transportation corridor.

North of Lake, the Midtown Greenway, a biking and hiking trail, was developed along the route of a largely abandoned rail line. At Lake's western end in Uptown, the Greenway sparked a real estate boom. Thousands of new apartments were built facing this linear green space. With its densely developed apartments, office buildings, and trendy restaurants, Uptown became a mini "downtown."

Originally, Minneapolis's largest body of water was named for US Secretary of War John C. Calhoun. But following a campaign by community activists who objected to the lake's connection with Calhoun, an outspoken supporter of slavery, the Minneapolis Park Board decided to eliminate that connection. The board renamed the lake Bde Maka Ska, the term used by the Dakota people who originally settled there. That change has been challenged in court by a group of South Minneapolis residents who want to retain the lake's original name. (Author's collection.)

In 2017, the Minneapolis Park Board gave Lola's Café a lease to operate a restaurant in the historic refectory building at Bde Maka Ska. Two years later, the refectory was destroyed in a fire, forcing Lola's to temporarily suspend its operation. For Lola's 2019 season, the cafe operated a food truck adjacent to the refectory site. (Author's collection.)

The first phase of the Midtown Greenway opened in 2000. Later phases completed the Greenway, a 5.7-mile biking and pedestrian pathway built along a railroad corridor paralleling Lake Street. At its western end, the greenway led to a real estate boom that brought several thousand new housing units to the Uptown and Lynlake districts. (Author's collection.)

The Uptown section of Lake Street is undergoing a development boom as mid-rise apartments and offices replace the district's older one and two-story buildings, some dating to the pre–World War I era. With its energy and dense development, Uptown is attracting residents and visitors who are looking for the ultimate urban experience. (Author's collection.)

Magers & Quinn, an independent bookstore, has been an Uptown fixture for the last 25 years. The store's building at 3038 Hennepin was originally a Chevrolet dealership dating to the early 1920s. From its modest origins in a small storefront near the University of Minnesota, Magers & Quinn has become one of the largest independent bookstores in the Midwest. (Author's collection.)

The current Walker Library opened in 2014 on the site of the former underground library named for Minneapolis civic leader T.B. Walker. The 2014 building was designed to serve a community meeting space for Uptown. It features floor to ceiling windows looking out at the Hennepin and Lagoon Avenues intersection, and roof monitors designed to capture sunlight. (Author's collection.)

In 2012, the Lake Street Council installed a series of permanent historical markers at three sections of Lake Street. Known collectively as the Museum in the Street, the markers offer Lake Street visitors an opportunity for self-guided walking tours in Uptown, Midtown, and East Lake. At each of its roughly 60 locations, the Museum in the Street provides brief histories of the site in English and Spanish. (Author's collection.)

Wing Young Huie's Lake Street USA exhibition represented the culmination of Huie's four-year effort to photograph everyday life along the Lake Street corridor. The exhibition, mounted in 2000, displayed 675 photographs in storefronts and community spaces along the corridor. Huie has said that the photographs enabled him to see something he would not normally see: how people live day to day. (Author's collection.)

The Jungle Theater has made Lake Street and Lyndale Avenue its home since 1991. According to the theater's website, the Jungle "creates courageous, resonant theater that challenges, entertains and sparks expansive conversation." During its 30-year history, the Jungle has showcased theatrical work by new and emerging playwrights. (Author's collection.)

The sign on this building may indicate that it is a bowling alley, but bowling is only one of the offerings at this unique Lake Street venue. Bryant-Lake Bowl is also a restaurant, bar, and cabaret-style theater. (Author's collection.)

Schatzlein Saddle Shop celebrated its 100th anniversary in 2007. During that centennial year, the family's third generation, grandchildren of the store's founder, Emil Schatzlein, posed for the photograph above. Today, the Schatzlein family still operates the landmark Lake Street business. (Both, courtesy of Schatzlein Saddle Shop.)

Safari reflects the cosmopolitan nature of Lake Street's emerging business community. While the Fourth Avenue and Lake Street restaurant specializes in contemporary Somali cuisine, its menu shows the influence of a broad range of cultures from Europe, Africa, and the Middle East. Safari's event center serves as a popular community gathering spot. (Author's collection.)

Allina Health's decision to locate its corporate headquarters in the Midtown Exchange helped spur the redevelopment of the former Sears complex. A Minneapolis-based nonprofit, Allina operates a network of hospitals and clinics throughout Minnesota and western Wisconsin. The corporation's flagship facility, Abbott Northwestern Hospital, is adjacent to the Midtown Exchange. (Both, courtesy of Ray Harris.)

The idea for an internationally themed market on Lake Street took shape in the early 2000s when local community leaders faced the prospect of a big-box retail development at the Sears site. A group of nonprofit community organizations came together to create the Global Market as an alternative to a national retail chain development at the site. (Author's collection.)

The market provides affordable space where local entrepreneurs are able to grow their businesses. Global Market businesses are able to take advantage of support services provided by several nonprofit lenders, including the Metropolitan Consortium of Community Developers, the Latino Economic Development Center, and the Neighborhood Development Center. The nonprofit groups provide business consulting and affordable financing. (Author's collection.)

After he closed Roberts Shoes in 2004, Mark Simon continued to own the building at Lake Street and Chicago Avenue that had housed his family's shoe store since 1937. In May 2018, a fire destroyed the building and displaced its tenants, many of whom were artists and small business owners. The building was something of a literary landmark. The well-known author Robert Pirsig wrote *Zen and the Art of Motorcycle Maintenance* while living in the Roberts Shoes building in 1974. (Courtesy of the Lake Street Council.)

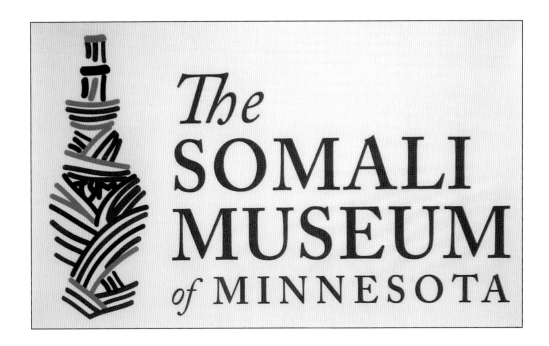

When it was founded in 2011, the Somali Museum of Minnesota was the country's only repository of Somali arts and culture. Today, the museum interprets the Somali world to the broader American community. The nonprofit organization sponsors a Somali dance group that performs traditional dances to audiences throughout Minnesota. (Both, courtesy of Hennepin County Library Special Collections.)

During its 20-year history, the Mercado Central has served as an incubator for Latino businesses in the Twin Cities. The Mercado was established in 1999 when Latino community leaders partnered with local nonprofit organizations to purchase and rehab this 20,000-square-foot building at Bloomington Avenue and Lake Street. The Mercado businesses have formed a cooperative that owns and operates their shared space. (Both, courtesy of Hennepin County Library Special Collections.)

This innovative arts organization was founded in 1973, when it was known as the Powderhorn Puppet Theater. In 1979, the group changed its name to In the Heart of the Beast Puppet and Mask Theater. In 1987, the nonprofit arts group purchased and renovated the former Avalon Theater for its permanent home. The theater's May Day parades have been popular community events. (Left, author's collection; below, Hennepin County Public Library Special Collections.)

Shoppers line up outside Ingebretsen's butcher shop during the weeks leading up to Christmas. Many are there to buy Swedish meatballs, potato sausage, and other Scandinavian delicacies. Others shop for lutefisk, the reconstituted dried cod that many Minnesotans love to hate. During the holiday season, Ingebretsen's sells more lutefisk than any other retailer in the Twin Cities. (Both, courtesy of Minnesota Historical Society.)

The Minneapolis YWCA's Midtown branch opened in 2000 at Lake Street and Twenty-First Avenue. The Midtown facility includes a 100,000-square-foot health and fitness center equipped with an indoor swimming pool and indoor running track. Community members are able to access the fitness center by becoming YWCA members. (Author's collection.)

When the Hiawatha Light Rail line, later renamed the Blue Line, opened in 2004, its Lake Street Station served as a key transfer point for the Twin Cities' area-wide transit system. The new LRT station helped boost Lake Street's role as a major transportation corridor. The popular 21A bus line, which follows the route of the original Selby-Lake streetcar, connects with the Blue Line LRT at Lake Street. (Both, author's collection.)

For its recent summer seasons, the Midtown Farmers Market has relocated to a temporary site on the 3000 block of Minnehaha Avenue, adjacent to Moon Palace Books. When L and H Station, the Hennepin County development at Lake and Hiawatha, is completed, the market will have a permanent home on a public plaza at that site. (Both, author's collection.)

In November 2017, Moon Palace Books moved to a new building down the street from its original location on Minnehaha Avenue. The bookstore's new home is an 8,000-square-foot former warehouse with room for 15,000 books, a café, and an event space for parties and concerts. Moon Palace's expanded location is helping to promote the resurgence of independent book stores in the Twin Cities. (Both, author's collection.)

The remodeled East Lake Library, which opened in 2007, incorporated the original 1970s structure in the updated design. The $4 million remodeling added 25,000 square feet of new floor space to the building by smoothing out the original building's wedge shape. As part of the library's upgrades, the front entrance was moved closer to Lake Street, and a back entrance opening on to parking lot was added to the building. (Both, author's collection.)

Soderberg's history extends to 1924, when Harold and Mildred Soderberg opened their first florist shop at Twenty-Seventh Avenue and Lake Street. In 1935, they moved to a new location with a storefront and greenhouse at 3305 East Lake. Soderberg's has continued to do business there for more than 80 years. (Author's collection.)

Hymie's Vintage Records has been able to ride the recent vinyl resurgence. The business was established in 1968, decades before the era of iTunes and downloads. Hymie's continues to have one of the area's largest inventories of vinyl records. (Author's collection.)

Northern Sun Merchandising manufactures and sells t-shirts, buttons, and posters that champion progressive causes. The business, which began as a kitchen table operation in 1970, now serves a national market. Northern Sun is housed in the former East Lake Library building.

The façade of the El Lago Theater at Thirty-Fifth Avenue and East Lake Street has been preserved, at least in part, even though the building has not been used as a movie theater for 50 years. Architectural historian Larry Millett has described the El Lago as a "brick, stone terra cotta and tile fantasy from the 1920s rendered in an exotic mix of Baroque, Classical and Moorish Revival." In recent times, the theater building has housed a church. (Author's collection.)

The Hook and Ladder Theater is a performance and entertainment venue in the historic Fire Station 21 building at Lake Street and Minnehaha Avenue. The theater is operated by the nonprofit Firehouse Performance Arts Company (FPAC) in the space formerly occupied by Patrick's Cabaret. FPAC describes itself as a "mission driven arts organization and performance space that welcomes all artistic genres." (Author's collection.)

Milkweed Café now occupies the former home of the Blue Moon, one of Lake Street's oldest coffee shops, which opened in 1994. The café's new owners, Brenda Ingersoll and Alex Needham, are former Blue Moon staffers. Their coffee shop features fair trade artisan coffee and gluten-free baked goods. (Above, author's collection; below, courtesy of Milkweed Café.)

Merlins Rest has brought a touch of the British Isles to its corner of South Minneapolis. The Lake Street pub features live music and one of the Twin Cities' largest collections of single malt scotch whiskey. Along with American-style pub grub, Merlin's menu offers such traditional British comfort food as fish and chips and bangers and mash. (Author's collection.)

The Hi-Lo moved an authentic 1950s-era diner from Pennsylvania to Minneapolis to serve as its Lake Street restaurant. The South Minneapolis eatery, which opened in 2017, specializes in hearty breakfasts served all day long. Its name is an abbreviation of two local neighborhoods: Hiawatha and Longfellow. (Author's collection.)

This sculpture topped with a bronze flame serves as the focal point for the plaza at West River Commons, a mixed-use development at Lake Street and West River Parkway. The sculpture was created by Minneapolis artists Andrea Myklebust and Stanton Sears. The plaza marks Lake Street's eastern terminus at the Mississippi River. (Author's collection.)

DISCOVER THOUSANDS OF LOCAL HISTORY BOOKS FEATURING MILLIONS OF VINTAGE IMAGES

Arcadia Publishing, the leading local history publisher in the United States, is committed to making history accessible and meaningful through publishing books that celebrate and preserve the heritage of America's people and places.

Find more books like this at
www.arcadiapublishing.com

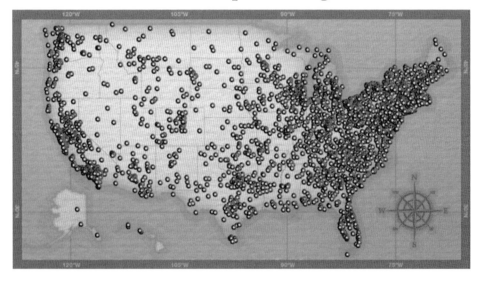

Search for your hometown history, your old
stomping grounds, and even your favorite sports team.

Consistent with our mission to preserve history on a local level, this book was printed in South Carolina on American-made paper and manufactured entirely in the United States. Products carrying the accredited Forest Stewardship Council (FSC) label are printed on 100 percent FSC-certified paper.

MADE IN THE